A CHILD'S
GREAT

Thomas Tapper

Volume I:

Bach
Beethoven
Mozart
Verdi
Liszt
Schumann

Published by Values-Driven®
(www.valuesdrivenpublishing.com)

PUBLISHER'S NOTE: These volumes were originally created as "activity books" which children could complete and bind themselves. Since they are here published in paperback version, all references to this formatting have been eliminated. This does not, however, affect the overall content of the book.

Contents

Bach:
The Story of the Boy Who Sang in the Streets

This is the house in which JOHANN SEBASTIAN BACH was born.

THE HOUSE IN WHICH BACH WAS BORN

This house stands in the town of Eisenach in Germany. It looks very much the same today as it did when Sebastian was a little boy. Many people go there to visit this house because the little boy grew to be a famous man.

In Eisenach there is a statue of Bach near the palace.

STATUE OF BACH AT EISENACH

In the same town in which Sebastian was born there stands on the top of a hill a very famous castle built many hundreds of years ago.

This castle is called the Wartburg.

THE CASTLE AT WARTBURG

As a boy little Sebastian used to climb the hill with his friends, and they, no doubt, had a happy time playing about the castle grounds. In one of its great halls the minstrels of Germany held their Song Contests.

When Sebastian was old enough he used to travel afoot, just as the minstrels did; his purpose was to go to hear fine organ players. Once as he sat weary by the roadside someone threw a herring to him so that he might eat as he rested.

BACH EATING THE HERRING

Little Sebastian's father was named JOHANN AMBROSIUS BACH. He, too, was a musician, as his people had been for many years.

JOHANN AMBROSIUS BACH

One of these was a miller who played and sang while the corn was grinding. His name was Veit Bach, and his little boy was called Hans, the Player, because he, too, loved to play the violin.

VEIT BACH AND HIS SON HANS

When Sebastian was ten years old his father and mother died. So he went to live with his brother, whose home was a few miles away.

Of this brother Sebastian had music lessons, and he improved so rapidly that he used to beg to be allowed to play the pieces in a big book in the library.

But the brother refused him this pleasure. However, little Sebastian was eager to learn all the music he could find, so he used to sit up on moonlight nights and copy these pages while his brother was asleep.

But what do you think happened when he had copied everything in that big book?

His brother found out what he had done and took all his precious music away from him.

BACH COPYING MUSIC BY MOONLIGHT

If you know any boy who is about twenty years old you may say to him, Bach was as old as you are when Benjamin Franklin was born in Boston.

And although there was this difference of twenty years or so in their ages, we may think of them at work in the world at the same time. You must remember that all men like Franklin and Bach who became famous did so by working very hard.

BENJAMIN FRANKLIN

Franklin, too, was born very poor. Once he walked the streets of Philadelphia with a loaf of bread under each arm. But by being faithful in all he did he became the friend of all his countrymen and of Kings and Queens besides.

11

Benjamin Franklin was quite a little younger than Sebastian Bach. But there was a famous man who was almost exactly Sebastian's age. This man composed an Oratorio that is loved by everybody. It is sung in cities and towns all over the world, particularly at Christmas time.

Do you happen to know the name of this Oratorio? If not, you can surely learn it by asking someone or by looking it up in a book.

The composer of the Oratorio is pictured below.

The Oratorio was first sung in the Irish city of Dublin, 1742.

At that time Sebastian Bach was living in Leipsic and had been for many years at the head of the Thomas School. He was known as its Cantor. Bach worked very hard here to supply music for several of the Leipsic churches, and he worked so well that his fame spread until it reached the ears of the Emperor.

Frederick the Great was also a musician and composer. So he invited Sebastian Bach to visit him at his castle. There were many people present, but Sebastian Bach was the principal guest. He played on many of the Emperor's fine pianos. When he reached home again he composed a musical work and dedicated it to the Emperor.

BACH PLAYING BEFORE FREDERICK THE GREAT

The kind of a piano that Sebastian Bach played on was not called a piano in his day. It was called a Clavier or Clavichord.

13

Some day you will study a collection of pieces by Sebastian Bach which was written for this instrument and was called *The Well-Tempered Clavichord*.

This is the kind of piano, or clavichord, that Bach used.

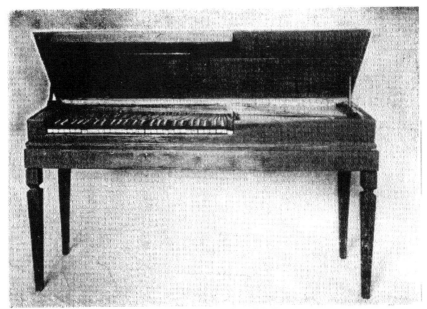

THE CLAVICHORD

And here is the beginning of the very first piece in the collection of which we have just spoken in Bach's handwriting.

BACH'S HANDWRITING

MORNING PRAYERS IN THE HOME OF
JOHANN SEBASTIAN BACH

Sebastian Bach had a very large family, twenty children altogether. Two of them studied music faithfully with their father.

One was Friedmann, for whom the father wrote a book called *Little Preludes*. Friedmann's brother, Philipp Emanuel Bach, was a very fine clavichord player. He wrote a book about music and composed many pieces.

WILLIAM FRIEDMANN BACH

15

PHILIPP EMANUEL BACH

Sebastian Bach died in 1750. He was sixty-five years of age.

Benjamin Franklin was at that time forty-four years old and George Washington was eighteen.

This is the way Bach wrote his name.

FACTS ABOUT SEBASTIAN BACH

Read these facts about Sebastian Bach and try to write his story out of them, using your own words.

When your story is finished ask your mother or your teacher to read it.

1. Full name: Johann Sebastian Bach.

2. Born 1685, died 1750.

3. As a little boy he sang in the streets, begging from door to door.

4. His father and mother died when he was ten years old.

5. He went to live with his brother.

6. He took his first position when he was seventeen.

7. He used to walk long distances to hear famous organists, one of whom was named Buxtehude.

8. He could play the organ, clavichord, violin, and other stringed instruments.

9. He wrote music for the voice (solo and chorus).

10. And for many different instruments.

11. He never met his fellow countryman, Handel.

12. Bach copied lots of music because printed music was dear in his day.

13. He was Cantor of the Thomas School for many years.

14. Once he visited Frederick the Great at Potsdam.

15. For his little son, Friedmann, he wrote a book of *Little Preludes*.

SOME QUESTIONS

1. In what year did Bach die?

2. Name an American who was alive at the same time.

3. What famous castle can be seen from the streets of Eisenach?

4. What other great German composer lived in Bach's time?

5. What instruments could Bach play?

6. For what purpose did Bach travel from place to place, as a boy?

7. What was the name of Sebastian's father?

8. Who was Hans, the Player?

9. Were any of Bach's children musical?

10. What music by Bach have you heard?

Beethoven:
The Story of a Little Boy Who Was Forced to Practice

Ludwig van Beethoven was born in the lovely town of Bonn, on the River Rhine, December 16, 1770.

The house in which he spent his boyhood is still standing. We see in the picture what a pretty, homelike place the house and the yard must have been. It is now the Beethoven House, or Museum, filled with mementos of the great composer. There you may see music pages written by him, letters, medals, instruments; even his ear trumpet is there.

THE BEETHOVEN HOUSE

Beethoven's father was a singer at the Chapel of the Elector. He was not a good father, for he did not care to work even enough to make his family comfortable. But the mother loved her boy with all her heart, as we shall see.

BEETHOVEN'S FATHER

Ludwig was only four years old when he began to study music. Like children of to-day he shed many a tear over the first lessons. In the beginning his father taught him piano and violin, and forced him to practice. At school he learned, just as we do to-day, reading, writing, arithmetic, and later on, Latin.

THE FIRST LESSON

Never again after thirteen, did Ludwig go to school for he had to work and earn his living.

Do you wonder what kind of a boy he was?

We are told that he was shy and quiet. He talked little and took no interest in the games that his boy and girl companions played.

While Ludwig was in school he played at a concert for the first time. He was then eight years old. Two years later he had composed quite a number of pieces. One of these was printed. It was called *Variations on Dressler's March*. On the title page of this piece it said:—

VARIATIONS ON DRESSLER'S MARCH
Composed by a Young Amateur
LOUIS VAN BEETHOVEN
Aged ten years. 1780

Then the little boy studied with a teacher named Christian Gottlob Neefe, who took real interest in him. Neefe did not, as was said of Beethoven's father, punish the little boy severely to keep him at his practice, hour after hour.

Often when Neefe had to travel Ludwig took his teacher's place as organist at the Court. Then with the organ lessons there were other lessons in Harmony. So rapidly did the boy improve that his teacher said one day:

"If he goes on as he has begun, he will someday be a second Mozart."

Our young hero of thirteen was surely busy every hour of the day. He played in an orchestra, as accompanist. He gave lessons, played the organ in church, studied the violin, and kept up his work in composition. He always kept a note-book for musical ideas.

Most every child in these days has more and better opportunities than had the great Beethoven when he was a child. Here is a picture of the funny old organ in the Minorite Church of Bonn upon which Beethoven played when he was a little boy.

BEETHOVEN'S ORGAN

Look at the funny stops at the top and compare it with the best organ in your own town. This is little better than a toy beside our fine organs of to-day,—yet it was the best that Beethoven had to practice upon. When Neefe said that he would probably be a second Mozart the words filled Ludwig with a great desire. On his sixteenth birthday what do you think happened? Why, he set out from Bonn to Vienna, where Mozart lived.

But scarcely had he begun to feel at home in Vienna when news came to him that his mother was ill. She had always been a good mother, kind of heart, great of hope for her little boy, and probably she sympathized with the hard lot that made him have to work so early in life. When he learned of her sickness he hastened to Bonn.

Who was happier, he said to one of his friends, than I, so long as I was able to speak the sweet name of Mother and know that she heard me?

BEETHOVEN'S MOTHER

Vienna had given him a wonderful happiness. He met Mozart and had some lessons from him in composition. When he played for the great master, Mozart tip-toed from the room and said softly to those present:

"Pay heed to this boy. He will surely make a noise in the world someday."

BEETHOVEN AND MOZART

After his Mother's death he determined that he would remain there. And it was not until he talked with Joseph Haydn, who stopped at Bonn on his way to London, that he decided once more to journey to Vienna.

JOSEPH HAYDN

Beethoven was twenty-two years old at the time he met Papa Haydn. Beethoven showed the master some of his compositions. Haydn urged him to go at once to Vienna, promising to give him lessons in composition on his return from London.

Everywhere in Vienna Beethoven was a welcome guest. He was proud (but in the right way), very honest, always straightforward and independent. But, like his mother, he was warm-hearted and as true as could be. There was nothing in his nature that was mean, or cruel, or wrong in any way. He took pride in his talent and worked hard to perfect himself in it.

Here is what Beethoven's handwriting looked like.

BEETHOVEN'S HANDWRITING

Bit by bit, the great power of Beethoven as a pianist became known. He played much among his friends, but he did not like to perform in public.

A story is told that once he was to play his C major Concerto at a concert. When he arrived at the hall he found the piano was tuned so low that he had to play the Concerto in C# major.

You know how hard it is to transpose a simple piece, but think of transposing a Concerto and playing it with orchestra without time for practice!

Do you sometimes wonder what the great composer looked like? Beethoven lived outside of Vienna and often took long walks in the country. Once a little boy ten years of age was taken by his father to visit Beethoven. The boy must have been a very observant boy for he wrote out a description of how Beethoven looked. This is the little boy's picture as a man:

CARL CZERNY

And this is the description he gave of Beethoven:

"Beethoven was dressed in a dark gray jacket and trousers of some long-haired material, which reminded me of the description of Robinson Crusoe I had just been reading. The jet-black hair stood upright on his head. A beard, unshaven for several days, made still darker his naturally swarthy face. I noticed also, with a child's quick perception, that he had cotton wool which seemed to have been dipped in some yellow fluid in both ears. His hands were covered with hair, and the fingers were very broad, especially at the tips."

You know, of course, that when we think of music we think of *hearing* it. We think how it *sounds* to us. A lover of music loves to hear its *tones* and to feel its *rhythm*.

Like every other human being, Beethoven loved music in just this way. He loved its sounds as they fell on the ear. As colors delight our eyes, so tones fell with delight upon the ears of this man.

Beethoven was once invited to play at the home of a nobleman, but upon being informed that he would be expected to go as a menial, he indignantly rejected the proposal.

THE ANGRY BEETHOVEN

Beethoven had many friends and was fond of them. They knew that he was a genius and were glad to forget some of the very strange things that he did when he got angry. Here is a picture of the great master seated among a group of his friends. Although Beethoven was odd, his friends loved him.

BEETHOVEN PLAYING FOR HIS FRIENDS

But a strange fate touched him and took away his sense of hearing. From the time he was about thirty years old his hearing grew gradually worse. Indeed it was necessary for him to have a piano especially constructed with additional wires so that he could hear.

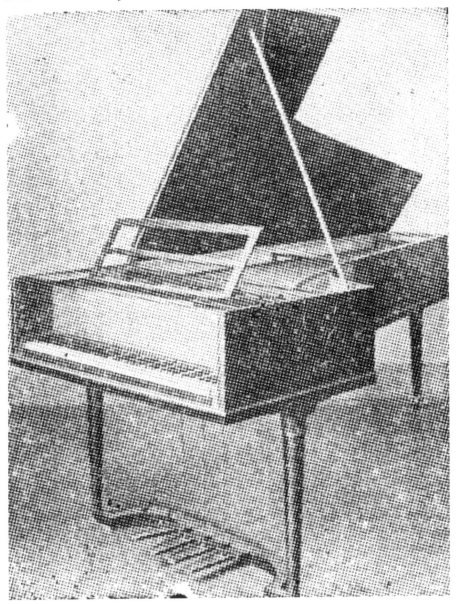

BEETHOVEN'S PIANO

Can you think of anything more cruel, more terrible, more depressing, more awful?

BEETHOVEN IN THE COUNTRY

And yet he went on day, after day, composing beautiful music as he walked the fields, or as he sat at his table. For we must remember that he could hear his own music in his thoughts. That is, the mind that made the music could hear it, though the ear itself was forever closed to the sound of it.

Year after year he continued to write symphonies and concertos, sonatas, songs, choral and chamber music.

And year after year the poor ears closed a little more and still a little more, until finally not even the loudest noises could penetrate them.

And yet he worked bravely; writing every beautiful music thought that came to him, so that the world, and that means you and all of us, might have them. When Beethoven was dying in 1827, Schubert called upon him and remained with him for some time.

BEETHOVEN AND SCHUBERT

SOME FACTS ABOUT BEETHOVEN

Read these facts about Ludwig van Beethoven and try to write his story out of them, using your own words.

When your story is finished ask your mother or your teacher to read it.

1. The composer's full name was Ludwig van Beethoven.

2. He was born at Bonn on the River Rhine. (Look for Bonn on the map.)

3. His birthday is December 16, and his birth year was 1770.

4. The Beethoven House is now a Museum.

5. Beethoven's father was a singer.

6. Ludwig began to study music at the age of four.

7. He was shy and quiet in school, always thinking even then of music.

8. Even as a little boy he composed music.

9. When he was ten years old his first published composition appeared.

10. A teacher who helped him very much was Christian Gottlob Neefe.

11. Beethoven learned to play several instruments.

12. He went to Vienna when he was sixteen, met Mozart and had lessons from him.

13. Later, Beethoven met Haydn at Bonn.

14. On Haydn's advice he returned to Vienna, making it his home for the rest of his life.

15. Carl Czerny once called on Beethoven and wrote a fine description of him.

16. At about thirty Beethoven became deaf.

17. Most of the great symphonies were composed after he lost his hearing.

18. Beethoven died March 26, 1827, at the age of 57.

SOME QUESTIONS

1. When and where was Beethoven born?

2. Who was his first teacher?

3. What did his father do?

4. How long did little Ludwig go to school?

5. What description of him as a boy in school has been given?

6. How old was he when he first played in public?

7. What composition of his was first to be published?

8. Which of his teachers took great interest in him?

9. What did he say about the little boy's future?

10. Where did Beethoven go when he was sixteen years old?

11. With what two great masters did he study?

12. What composer, as a little boy, went to see Beethoven?

13. How did he describe him?

14. Name some of the forms of music which Beethoven composed.

15. Write a list of music by Beethoven that you have heard.

16. What is a concerto? a sonata?

17. How old was Beethoven when he died?

Mozart:
The Story of A Little Boy and His Sister Who Gave Concerts

The composer whom we call WOLFGANG AMADEUS MOZART was called Wolferl when he was a little boy.

He had a sister, MARIA ANNA, who was called NANNERL.

Nannerl was five years older than her brother. She had lessons from her father on a kind of piano called a harpsichord.

Here is a picture of one.

MOZART'S HARPSICHORD

When Wolferl was three years old he used to listen to Nannerl's playing. He always watched and listened when Papa Mozart gave her a harpsichord lesson.

Little as he was, he would often go to the harpsichord and try to pick out tunes with his chubby fingers. His father noticed that Wolferl could remember quite a little of the music that Nannerl was practising.

And here is a picture of Wolferl trying to reach the keys so as to play the melody of his sister's lesson.

THE INFANT MOZART AT THE PIANO

When Wolferl was four years old he began to take lessons.

While he practised no one ever spoke to him because he was so serious about it. If other children came to play with Nannerl he would make music for their games and marching; playing in strict time all the while.

Here is Nannerl's picture when she grew up to be a young lady.

MOZART'S SISTER

Father Mozart loved both of his children deeply and often played with them. The violin was the instrument he liked best and little Mozart had

40

daily lessons in his home. Here we see him playing while his sister sings.

A MOZART FAMILY TRIO

In this picture we see Papa Mozart, who was a very fine player on the violin. Wolferl and Nannerl are playing the piano.

MOZART PLAYING WITH HIS FATHER AND SISTER

When Wolferl was nearly six his father took him and Nannerl on a concert tour. Everybody wanted to hear them play and they gave many concerts.

Wolferl spent all his boyhood with his music. He went to many places to play, even as far from Salzburg, in Austria (where he was born), as to Paris and London.

Everywhere he went people were happy to see him and his sister and to hear them play. And they, too, were happy to play because they loved the music so much.

When they reached Vienna they played for the Emperor and Empress.

When Wolferl was presented to the Empress he jumped up into her lap and kissed her.

Wolferl was always busy composing music. But he played games and had a good time just like any other boy. When he was busy with his music, however, he never let his thoughts go to anything else.

But we must not go too fast, for we want to see how Wolferl is growing up.

MOZART AT FIVE

Here is his picture when he was five years old and another when he was eight years old. Do you see his wig and sword?

MOZART AT EIGHT

Everybody in Paris wanted to hear Wolferl play when they knew that he had come, so they asked him to read at sight; to play the bass part to a melody and to accompany a song without seeing the music.

People also took great delight in asking him to play on the harpsichord with a cloth stretched over the keyboard so that he could not see the keys.

They all went to London to play for the King. The King wanted to see for himself how skillful little Mozart was, so he gave him pieces by Bach and Handel to play at sight. Mozart read them off at once. Here is a fine picture of the Mozart children when they played for the King and the Queen.

MOZART AT THE COURT OF THE EMPEROR

It must have been very fine for a little boy of seven to play for kings and queens. But Wolferl was not spoiled by it all. He was just a happy-hearted boy all the time.

He always made it a rule to put his mind on what he was doing and do it the very best he knew how.

It is just as good a rule now as it was when he was alive.

It is time now that we learned the birthday of Mozart. If we think of it every year on the 27th of January, it will be easy to remember it.

In what year was he born?

Here is another picture of Mozart in 1766. How old was he then? (Beethoven was born four years afterward.)

MOZART IN 1766

When anyone is always busy at one thing he soon gets a lot done. As Wolferl grew and kept on writing music all the time he made a great many pieces. Some were short like a song, others were long like an opera. He wrote for the piano, the violin and the voice. And he composed operas, symphonies and ever so many other kinds of music.

Mozart liked to be alone when he was working upon his compositions. He used to go to a little house on the edge of Vienna and lock himself in. The people of the city of Salzburg, in Austria, took this house long after Mozart's death and moved it to a park where all may go to see it, just as we in America go to see the houses of William Penn, Lincoln and Washington.

45

WHERE MOZART COMPOSED

Can you remember, without turning back, the year in which Mozart was born?

Some other great musicians were alive at that time. And during his lifetime some were born who became great men.

In the year when Mozart was born both Handel and Haydn were living. And Haydn lived eighteen years after Mozart's death.

You can remember it by these lines:

1732	The years of Haydn's life	1809
	1756 The years of Mozart's life 1791	

When Mozart was fourteen years old Beethoven was born. Mozart knew him and he knew Papa Haydn also, and they were very good friends.

In our own country there lived in Mozart's lifetime Benjamin Franklin and three Presidents of the United States—George Washington, John Adams and Thomas Jefferson.

I wonder if Washington ever heard of Mozart?

Perhaps we can best keep all these names together by looking at this page now and again.

1706 Benjamin Franklin was born.

1732 Washington and Haydn were born.

1736 Patrick Henry was born.

1743 Thomas Jefferson was born.

1750 Bach died.

1756 WOLFGANG AMADEUS MOZART was born.

1759 Handel died.

1770 Beethoven was born.

1771 Walter Scott was born.

1790 Franklin died.

1791 Mozart died.

1809 Joseph Haydn died.

Isn't it fine to think of Mozart writing so much music, so many operas, symphonies and sonatas; traveling so much, meeting so many people and never being spoiled by it all.

While he wrote many very great pieces of music, here is something he composed when he was five years old. He made up the pieces at the piano and his father wrote them down note for note in a little copy book.

FACTS ABOUT MOZART

Read these facts about Wolfgang Amadeus Mozart and try to write his story out of them, using your own words. When your story is finished, ask your mother or your teacher to read it.

1. Full name: Wolfgang Amadeus Mozart.

2. Born Jan. 27, 1756; died Dec. 5, 1791.

3. The sister's name was Maria Anna.

4. Maria Anna was five years older than Wolfgang.

5. The pet names of the children were Wolferl and Nannerl.

6. Little Mozart loved to hear his sister play.

7. He started to study when he was four.

8. Mozart went on a concert tour with his sister when he was six years old.

9. When he was a child he visited many great cities, among them Paris, London and Vienna.

10. Handel and Haydn were living when Mozart was born.

11. Benjamin Franklin, George Washington, Patrick Henry, Thomas Jefferson and Walter Scott were all alive during the time of Mozart.

12. Mozart was five years old when he wrote his first piece.

SOME QUESTIONS

1. In what country was Mozart born?

2. In what city was Mozart born?

3. Where did Mozart play before the Emperor and the Empress?

4. Did Mozart play games and have a good time like other boys?

5. Why did people ask Mozart to play upon the harpsichord with a cloth stretched over the keys?

6. Whose compositions did the King of England ask Mozart to play?

7. What great American patriot was born in the same year as Haydn?

8. Which lived the longer life, Haydn or Mozart?

9. Have you ever heard a piece by Mozart?

10. Was Mozart spoiled by meeting many people?

Verdi:
The Story of the Little Boy Who Loved the Hand Organ

The picture on this page is of the house wherein a great composer was born. Of course, one is not born a great composer. He has to become that. So, at the moment this story begins there is, within this house, a little boy quite like any other boy. He loved to play and to make a noise and to have a good time. But most of all—what do you think he loved?

A hand organ.

VERDI'S BIRTHPLACE

Whenever the organ man came into the village of Roncole, in Italy (where Verdi was born, October 10, 1813), he could not be kept indoors. But he followed the wonderful organ and the wonderful man who played it, all day long, as happy as he could be.

When Giuseppe was seven years old his father, though only a poor innkeeper, bought him a spinet, a sort of small piano. So faithfully did the little boy practice that the spinet was soon quite worn out and new jacks, or hammers, had to be made for it. This was done by Stephen Cavaletti, who wrote a message on one of the jacks telling that he made them anew and covered them with leather, and fixed the pedal, doing all for nothing, because the little boy, Giuseppe Verdi, showed such willingness to practice and to learn. Thus the good Stephen thought this was pay enough.

Here is a picture of the little piano. In Verdi's language (Italian) it is called a *spinetta*.

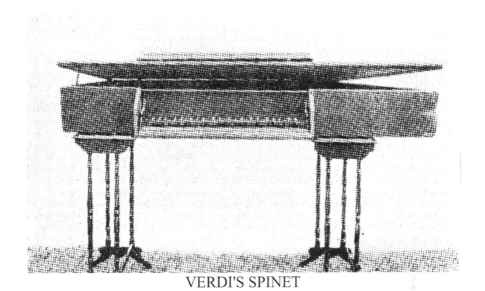

VERDI'S SPINET

It was on this spinet that the little boy discovered one day a wonderful chord, for so it seemed to him. It was this:

The tones delighted him and he pressed the keys over and over again to drink them in. But the next day when he sought again the keys which made the lovely sound, he could not find them. This made him so impatient and finally so curious that he began to break the spinet to pieces with a hammer. Fortunately the noise he made brought his father into the room and the spinet was saved.

When Giuseppe was making his first attempt to find beautiful chords on the spinet he was, as we have said, seven years old. That was in 1820.

When he was ten years old (what year was that?) Giuseppe became organist at the old church of Roncole. Truly a little boy for so great a position! One day he scratched his name on the woodwork. Here is a picture of the organ:

ORGAN AT RONCOLE

Here is the scratching of his name:

And here is the way he wrote his name, as a man:

Then there came the question of education—of reading, writing, spelling and arithmetic—for this music-loving boy. The Verdis wanted Giuseppe to grow up as he should; so it was arranged for him to go to school in the neighboring town of Busseto. A cobbler lived there who was a friend of the family, and with him Giuseppe went to live, having board, lodging and tuition at the school, and all for six cents a day.

Giuseppe still played the organ at Roncole, going thither afoot every Sunday morning and back after nightfall.

He must have been a weary little boy after the day's music-making at the church. One Sunday night when it was dark and he was too weary to notice where he was going, he fell into a ditch, from which he was rescued by an old woman, who, hearing his call for help, pulled the half-frozen boy out of the water.

Our little hero had another talent besides music. He knew how to win the friendship of people. So at Busseto a man named Barezzi offered to take him into his business. He sold spices, drugs and perfumes. But besides this he played the flute in the church. At his house Giuseppe heard lots of good music, for the town orchestra rehearsed there. Here is a picture of Giuseppe's friend:

BAREZZI

56

Then Giuseppe made another friend who gave him a wonderful bit of advice. HE URGED HIM TO BECOME A COMPOSER!

Better still he helped the boy in every way he could until he was sixteen years old. By that time our little Giuseppe was grown to be quite a man. His friend, whose name was Ferdinando Provesi, was proud of him, for already he was becoming a master. He played the cathedral organ at times; he conducted the Philharmonic Orchestra; he led its rehearsals, and he composed music for its concerts.

PROVESI

So you see—all the wonderful operas that were to come were already on the way!

It has been written that Provesi was the first person to see and understand Verdi's real genius. The boy worked hard and advanced so rapidly that it was soon necessary for him to go to a larger city for lessons.

Now a good friend is always a good friend, so it is pleasing to tell that Barezzi sent Giuseppe to Milan, the lovely city of Lombardy, to study. And here a curious thing happened. He was refused a scholarship at the Conservatory of Milan; the reason given was that the authorities considered him to show no special talent for music. But this made no difference to the boy. He believed in his talent and kept at work to perfect it.

VERDI AS A YOUNG MAN

So, as the years went by, he kept on learning more and more, doing his work well and always preparing himself for better things. Then one day he was ready to begin to compose the operas that made him famous.

Some time when you read the full list of Verdi's operas you will learn that he wrote thirty. The first was performed in 1839, when he was twenty-six years old, and the last in 1893, when he was eighty. You will not need to remember the titles of them all, but you must know the names of the great ones, for one day you will see and hear them performed.

VERDI IN OLD AGE

Here are the principal ones:

Ernani,	Rigoletto,	Il Trovatore,
La Traviata,	Sicilian Vespers,	Othello,
Aida,	Masked Ball,	Falstaff.

Do you know that of one of Verdi's operas the scene is laid in our country? The MASKED BALL was first entitled Gustavo III. But the authorities would not allow reference to certain political matters in it. Therefore the libretto (or story) of the opera was changed, and the scene laid in Boston, Massachusetts. One of the characters was the Governor of Boston, a humorous matter to us, for there never was any such official.

Another famous opera by Verdi, the scene of which is laid in a foreign country, is Aida. It was written for the Khedive of Egypt, and first performed in Cairo in 1871, when the composer was fifty-eight years old.

A SCENE FROM AÏDA

After Verdi had composed Aida he wrote no more operas for sixteen years. Then to the great surprise of all the world he wrote two others, the finest of them all—Othello and Falstaff.

Meanwhile he was a farmer. He planted, harvested, helped his tenants, urged them to cultivate the land carefully. He bought all kinds of American farming machinery to show the Italians how to cultivate the ground to best advantage.

The great man, who was once a simple little boy, died in 1901, on January 27, which day is the anniversary of Mozart's birth.

All his life long Verdi had succeeded, doing a little more and a little better each year, so that, at the end of his life, he was able to do a truly wonderful thing: namely, to build a home where musicians—who had not succeeded in life—could find a comfortable abiding place in their old age.

VERDI HOME FOR AGED MUSICIANS

In this House are many souvenirs of the great Italian. Here, too, is the tomb of Giuseppe Verdi.

VERDI'S TOMB

Verdi was loved by his fellow-countrymen. His music is their joy—and ours—and will so remain for years to come; perhaps forever.

The great sculptor, Vincenzo Gemito, has molded wonderful bronze busts of Verdi, which shows us how the little boy of Roncole grew to be a man of world renown.

SOME FACTS ABOUT GIUSEPPE VERDI

Read these facts about Giuseppe Verdi, and try to write his story out of them, using your own words.

When your story is finished, ask your mother or your teacher to read it.

1. Giuseppe Verdi was born in Roncole, Italy, October 10, 1813.

2. He began to learn the Spinet when he was seven years old.

3. The Spinet is an early form of the piano.

4. Among the great composers who were alive when Verdi was a little boy were: Beethoven, Schubert, Berlioz and Schumann.

5. He became organist at Roncole when he was ten years old (1823).

6. He went to school in Busseto and lived with a cobbler.

7. After a time he studied in Milan.

8. But not at the famous Milan Conservatory, for he was told there that he had no special talent for music.

9. Verdi wrote thirty operas.

10. The first was performed in 1839, when he was twenty-six years old.

11. One of his operas has its scene laid in Boston, Mass.

12. Another is about Egypt, and the scene is laid in Memphis and Thebes, in the time of the Pharaohs.

13. Verdi founded, for aged musicians, the Casa di Riposo (House of Rest).

14. Besides the thirty operas Verdi wrote a string quartet, The Manzoni Requiem, and a National Hymn.

15. For a period of sixteen years Verdi wrote no operas. Then he produced his two great works, Othello and Falstaff.

16. He died at St. Agatha, January 27, 1901.

SOME QUESTIONS

1. When and where was Verdi born?

2. How old was he when he died?

3. Can you mention three works of Verdi that are not operas?

4. How many operas can you name from memory?

5. What instruments did Verdi play as a boy?

6. What was the title of Verdi's first opera?

7. The title of his last two operas?

8. What did Verdi love to do besides compose music?

9. What is a Spinet?

10. In what famous city did he study as a boy?

11. How many operas, in all, did Verdi compose?

12. Where is the scene of Aida laid?

13. To what did Verdi devote his fortune?

Liszt: The Story of a Boy Who Became a Great Pianist and Teacher

This is the house in which was born a little boy who became a famous pianist and a great teacher. This house is in Raiding, in Hungary.

HOUSE IN WHICH FRANZ LISZT WAS BORN

Now-a-days there is a little tablet over the door, which tells us that Franz Liszt was born in this house, on the Twenty-second Day of October, 1811.

Do you remember that once upon a time Joseph Haydn lived as court musician in the Esterhazy family? He wore a tie wig and a wonderful bright uniform; for he was master of the music in that great house.

JOSEPH HAYDN

Now, long after Joseph Haydn's time, Adam Liszt, father of Franz, lived with the Esterhazy's. He was the family steward, having charge of all the property.

And, too, he loved music. So we may believe that he told his little boy, Franz, about the great master Haydn. For Adam Liszt was not only a lover of music but he gave his son his first lessons in piano playing. Liszt's mother was of German blood. She was born in lower Austria. Below are pictures of Liszt's mother and father.

LISZT'S MOTHER AND FATHER

Little Franz practiced so faithfully and so eagerly, I am sure, that when he was only nine years of age he gave a concert in public. He played so well that some good friends offered to send him to Vienna where he could continue his studies.

And so the little boy left home and began the studies that led him to become the greatest pianist of his time. His piano teacher was a man of whom almost everybody knows. Does he not have a round, good-natured face? And does he not look kind? Well, he could be severe when his pupil's lessons did not please him.

His name was Carl Czerny. Here is his picture.

CARL CZERNY

On New Year's day of the year that little Franz was eleven years old he played in public in Vienna. It must have been a wonderful occasion. All the great people were there; and among them was one who was greatest of all, Beethoven.

BEETHOVEN

Then Adam Liszt thought his boy should go to Paris. He wished him to become a student in the conservatory there. But its director, Cherubini, refused to admit Franz to the classes. So, like most of us, he studied with a private teacher. Also, he traveled to England and to all the countries of Europe, giving concerts. His fame was becoming greater and his playing was the delight of all who heard him. Here are two pictures of Franz as a boy. He dressed differently from boys of today. But do you not think his face is a fine one? Full of light and life and eagerness?

LISZT AS A BOY

Franz was only sixteen years old when his father died. They had been good comrades, had traveled together and talked with one another about music and musicians. The boy must have grieved keenly over the loss of so good and kind a companion as his father had been. But he went earnestly to work to earn a living for his mother and himself. He knew many famous people and we may be sure that everyone helped him. Here are two of Franz's friends of that time.

VICTOR HUGO - F. CHOPIN

AT THE PIANO

I am sure you will like to know how Liszt looked as he sat at the piano. Here he sits playing. You see he had only a simple kind of piano. But he mastered it so thoroughly that he could make people wonder at his art. That is what we learn from the lives of famous people. They are always true to their talent.

After Liszt had traveled many years over Europe (he never visited the United States), he became conductor at the Court Theatre at Weimar. This new music work interested him so much that he gave up travel as a concert pianist. He helped many composers by having their operas performed at the Weimar Theatre. Some of the operas that had their first performance there are now famous indeed.

Among these were "Lohengrin," "Tannhauser" and "The Flying Dutchman" by Richard Wagner.

R. WAGNER - R. SCHUMANN - F. SCHUBERT

Then there were "Genoveva" and "Manfred" by Robert Schumann. Also "Alfonzo and Estrella" by Franz Schubert was given. It would have delighted Schubert's heart if he could have heard this; but he, poor man, had died some years before.

Then Liszt did something else at Weimar that endeared him to hosts of pianists. He held classes and taught the secrets of his wonderful playing to those who were talented and could understand. He was the soul of generosity. When someone, who was gifted but could not pay, came for advice, he gave it freely. When concerts did not pay, he himself often took the loss so that others should not suffer.

Is it not wonderful to think of a man, so loved by the public, giving with such great generosity? Truly it is better to give than to receive.

LISZT AND SOME FAMOUS PUPILS
S. Liebling - Rosenthal - Liszt - Dora - Peterson
Siloti - Ans der Ohe - Sauer - Gottschlag
Friedheim - Reisenauer

All good and wonderful things live on forever. Even though Liszt moved from Weimar, spending his last years in Budapest, Rome and elsewhere, he was not idle. There was always a circle of people about him. And always his full-hearted, generous nature kept him at work for the good of others. He reminds us of Beethoven who once said,

75

"Composing is a capital thing. For instance if a friend is in distress and I have no money at hand to help him, I can sit down and compose something which I can sell and so relieve him." It seems that Franz Liszt thought the same for he was forever helping someone else.

We have already seen how Liszt looked as he sat at the piano. This is Liszt at the conductor's stand. Do you see his baton and the score on the desk? And the position of the left hand? When Liszt conducted the orchestra the players watched every movement of his hands and every look of his eyes so as to play just as he desired.

LISZT AS CONDUCTOR

Franz Liszt was kind to all people who came to him. There was one musician, however, for whom he did a great deal. You know him for he composed many operas. One of them is called "Parsifal." Another is "The Flying Dutchman." Here is his picture. Do you know his name?

Someday the operas of Richard Wagner will give you great pleasure.
At first they were not liked by the public. Wagner had few friends and
his life was very hard. But Franz Liszt believed in him and in his work.
And so he helped him.

At first Wagner did not like Liszt. He once said, "I never repeated my
first call on Liszt." By this he meant that he wished the acquaintance to
end. When Liszt realized that Wagner did not care to understand him,
he tried his best to keep the friendship secure. Liszt never wished to
misunderstand another human being. So, it was not long before
Wagner's opinion of Liszt changed, for he said, later, "Through the
love of this rarest friend I gained a real home for my art."

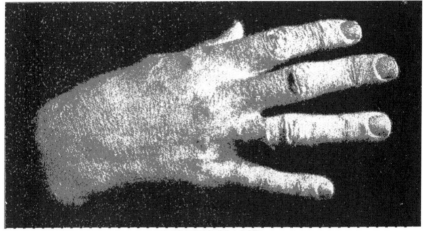

LISZT'S HAND

There is one thing true for us all. We carry our early thoughts along
with us all through life. The friends we make from youth and the
thoughts we think from youth are always at hand to bless us if we have
done wisely.

Once when little Franz was thirteen years old he played before the
English King, George IV. Sixty years later we see him again, once
more the guest of the English people.

It is pleasant to think of Liszt meeting again and again the friends of
his boyhood. When he went to England, on this occasion, he was quite
an old man. As he stepped out upon the stage to play, for the last time,
everybody, even the people outside of the hall, who could not get in,

78

shouted themselves hoarse. Those within rose to greet him with tears and cheers that are given only to the kings of the earth.

LISZT IN LATER LIFE

While we know of this artist chiefly as a great pianist, we shall learn, as we grow older, that he was a great composer as well. He wrote music for piano, for orchestra, for the voice. There are symphonies, masses, oratorios and cantatas. Once, as a boy, he met Franz Schubert in Vienna. In later years he arranged many of Schubert's songs in a truly beautiful way for the piano,—songs like the "Erl King," "Thou Art My Peace," "Hark, Hark the Lark."

So we may end by saying that Franz Liszt was a great man who remained simple and big-hearted all his life, and one whom the world loved for what he did.

No. 21

LISZT'S HAND WRITING

FACTS ABOUT FRANZ LISZT

Read these facts about Franz Liszt and try to make a story about him, in your own language.

When your story is done, and you have improved it all you can, copy it in pages 14, 15, and 16 of this book.

1. Franz Liszt was born in Raiding, in Hungary.

2. His birthday is October 22, 1811.

3. His father was his first teacher.

4. He studied piano in Vienna with Carl Czerny.

5. Then he went to Paris.

6. Among Liszt's boyhood friends were Beethoven, Schubert and Chopin.

7. After many years as a concert pianist, Liszt became opera conductor at Weimar.

8. He brought out many of the operas of Richard Wagner.

9. He was a great teacher of piano, and many people from Europe and from the United States studied with him.

10. He composed many fine works.

11. Among them are arrangements of many of Schubert's songs.

12. Liszt died in Rome in 1886. He was seventy-five years old.

13. Liszt wrote the life of his friend Frederic Chopin.

14. It has been said that no musician ever lived who did so much for others as Franz Liszt.

81

SOME QUESTIONS

1. When and where was Franz Liszt born?

2. Who was his first teacher?

3. What was his father's occupation? In what family did he live?

4. Where was his mother born?

5. With whom did Franz study piano in Vienna?

6. What famous musician did he meet in Vienna?

7. Name two or three people whom he met in Paris.

8. What great composer of opera did he assist?

9. Name some operas that Liszt produced at Weimar.

10. In what Italian city did Liszt live?

11. Whose songs did he arrange for piano?

12. What great musician's life was written by Franz Liszt?

13. When and where did Franz Liszt die?

Schumann: The Story of the Boy Who Made Pictures in Music

When Robert Schumann was a boy he used to amuse his friends by playing their pictures on the piano. He could make the music imitate the person.

One day he said to them: This is the way the farmer walks when he comes home singing from his work.

THE HAPPY FARME

Some day you will be able to play a lot of pieces by Schumann that picture the pleasantest things so clearly that you can see them very plainly indeed. In one of his books there is a music picture of a boy riding a rocking horse.

Another of a little girl falling asleep.

A March for Little Soldiers. (That is, make-believes.)

And then there are *Sitting by the Fireside, What they Sing in Church,* and a piece the first four notes of which spell the name of a composer who was a good friend of Schumann's.

This composer came from Denmark.

NIELS GADE

This is a picture of the house in Zwickau, Germany, where Robert Schumann was born.

SCHUMANN'S BIRTHPLACE.

Schumann was a strong healthy youth who had many friends and loved life.

SCHUMANN AS A YOUTH.

What do you think the Father and Mother of Robert Schumann wanted him to be when he was grown up?

A lawyer!

Robert was the youngest of five children, full of fun and up to all kinds of games. He went to school and became especially fond of reading plays.

He also loved to write little plays and to act them out on the stage that his Father had built for him in his room. So he and his companions could give their plays in their own theatre.

All the while Robert was taking piano lessons.

Just before he entered the High School he heard a pianist who played so beautifully that he made up his mind that he would become a musician.

The pianist whose playing gave him this thought is one whose name you will know better and better as you get older.

IGNACE MOSCHELES

There was lots of music-making in the Schumann home, for Robert and all his companions played and sang. And besides that, he composed music for them.

It must have been a pleasant picture to see all these German boys coming together to make music. If we could gather together some American boys who were alive at that same time, here are some we could have found:

Nathaniel Hawthorne, who wrote for children, *Tanglewood Tales* and the *Wonder Book*.

HAWTHORNE

Then there was Longfellow, who was born in Portland, Maine. How many of his poems do you know besides *Hiawatha*?

LONGFELLOW

And then we must not forget Whittier, who wrote many lovely poems. One was about a little girl who spelled the word that her companion missed in school and so she went above him in the class.

WHITTIER

And still there was another little boy only a year older than Robert Schumann. He was born in a cabin.

LINCOLN'S BIRTHPLACE

This boy's name, as you can guess, was Abraham Lincoln.

ABRAHAM LINCOLN

So when you think of Robert Schumann, let us also think of Hawthorne, Longfellow, Whittier, and Lincoln.

They were all doing their best, even as boys, to be useful.

Well, after all, Robert Schumann did not become a lawyer. He studied music very hard. His teacher was Frederick Wieck. His teacher's daughter, Clara Wieck, played the piano very beautifully.

CLARA WIECK

Papa Wieck, as he was called, was not very kind to Robert Schumann when the young man confessed that he and Clara loved one another and wished to marry.

FRIEDRICH WIECK

But after a while it all turned out happily and they were married. So Clara Wieck became Clara Schumann.

Here is a picture of them seated together.

ROBERT AND CLARA SCHUMANN

In the sixteen years that Robert Schumann lived after he and Clara Wieck were married he composed lots of music for the piano, besides songs, symphonies, and other kinds of compositions.

He was a teacher in the Leipzig Conservatory. Among his friends were Mendelssohn, Chopin, Brahms, and many others.

Schumann is best known as a composer of music, although he was also a teacher, a conductor, and a writer upon musical subjects. For many years he was the head of a musical newspaper, which is remembered to this day because of the great work he did in helping people to understand new music and find out new composers. When he was a very young man Schumann wanted to become a pianist, but he unfortunately used a machine that he thought was going to help him play better. It hurt his hand so that he was never able to play well again. Poor Schumann went out of his mind in his last years, and died insane, July 29, 1856.

CLARA SCHUMANN.

Clara Schumann lived forty years after Robert Schumann died. She was the teacher of many students, some of whom traveled from America to study with her. She, too, was a composer and a concert pianist who played in public from the time she was ten years of age.

FACTS ABOUT ROBERT SCHUMANN

1. Robert Schumann was born at Zwickau, in Saxony, Germany, on June 8, 1810.

2. When Schumann was nine years old he heard the great pianist Ignaz Moscheles play and resolved to become a great pianist.

3. When Schumann was a youth he showed a gift for writing poetry.

4. Schumann's father was a successful book-seller.

5. All through his life Schumann was a great lover of the writings of the German author, Jean Paul (whose full name was Jean Paul Richter). Much of his music shows his high regard for that writer of fairy stories.

6. Schumann was twenty-one years old when he injured his hand and learned that therefore he could not hope to be a pianist. It was then that he made up his mind to be a composer.

7. Schumann had enough means to live in comfort. He was not poor, as were Mozart, Schubert, and some others.

8. Robert and Clara Schumann had eight children, and some of Schumann's best music was written to interest his children.

9. Schumann died July 29, 1856.

SOME QUESTIONS ABOUT ROBERT SCHUMANN

When you can answer them, try to write the Story of Schumann.

1. In what country was Schumann born?

2. Can you name some pieces for the piano composed by Schumann?

3. What did he write when he was a little boy?

4. What great pianist did Robert hear when a boy?

5. Name some famous Americans who were boys when Robert was going to school.

6. Who wrote Hiawatha? Tanglewood Tales?

7. With whom did Robert Schumann study the piano?

8. Whom did Robert Schumann marry?

9. Tell what you know about her.

10. Where did Schumann teach?

11. Mention some of his friends.

12. What does the composer picture for us in the "Happy Farmer?"

13. Whose name is spelled by these notes?

14. In what year was Schumann born?

15. Through what was Schumann best known?

16. How did he help people find new composers?

17. What misfortune came to Schumann late in life?

The *Values-Driven* Homeschool Library

The **Values-Driven Homeschool Library** is published by Marc and Cindy Carrier and Values-Driven Publishing.

As homeschooling parents of eight children, we are always looking for resources that are

• Wholesome •
• Character-Building •
• Academically Excellent •
• Affordable •

With more and more modern books departing from the values-based teachings of yesteryear, we have utilized many vintage books in our homeschool.

Our goal is to equip homeschooling families for success and help them to maximize their time and financial resources by offering these quality resources in economical paperback editions.

Visit our Web site to view currently available titles:
www.ValuesDrivenFamily.com/homeschoollibrary

Made in the USA
San Bernardino, CA
14 April 2013